THE
LORD'S
SUPPER

POCKET ⟂ GUIDE

THE LORD'S SUPPER

F. LEVON HUCKS

ABINGDON PRESS
Nashville

THE LORD'S SUPPER

Copyright © 1992 by Abingdon Press

This book is printed on recycled, acid-free paper.

Library of Congress Cataloging-in-Publication Data

Hucks, F. Levon, 1953–
    The Lord's Supper   /   F. Levon Hucks.
      p.   cm.—(Pocket guide)
    "Pocket guide to the Lord's Supper."—T.p. verso.
    Includes bibliographical references.
    ISBN 0-687-22648-1 (alk. paper)
    1. Lord's Supper.   I. Title.   II. Title: Pocket guide to
the Lord's Supper.   III. Series: Pocket guide (Nashville,
Tenn.)
BV825.2.H83   1992   91-42514
234'.163—dc20   CIP

MANUFACTURED IN THE UNITED STATES OF AMERICA

ACKNOWLEDGMENTS

Many people have made contributions along the way which have helped in the completion of this project, but some of the most helpful contributions were made by Paula Sawyer and Evelyn Michele, who typed and retyped the manuscript.

I am, also, most grateful to Nancy Meffe, who read the manuscript and made helpful editorial suggestions during its preparation.

I would also like to thank the people at Abingdon Press, and especially Dr. Ronald P. Patterson, who has encouraged and guided me in bringing this project to the light of day. Many thanks to these and all the others who go unnamed.

To my wife, Darlene, and
to our children Erin, Warren,
Megan, and Nathan,
my school of theology.
And to my parents,
Fladger V. and Maxine J. Hucks

CONTENTS

CONTENTS

Foreword

Some time ago, when I was working on an academic degree, I was given an assignment by one of my professors which I was to carry out in the local church I was serving. I was instructed to ask twelve people from my church these two questions: What is the mission of the church and, What are the basic tasks the church must do to fulfill that mission?

The persons I interviewed said that the mission of the church was to reach people with the gospel. The basic tasks of the church ranged from evangelism to loving one another to preaching, teaching, and studying the Bible. Perhaps it was because of some reading I was doing at the time about Martin Luther's view of the sacraments, but I noticed in the responses that no one mentioned worship or the sacraments as part of the mission or task of the church. Worship seemed to be consumed in that task called "preaching." I am a Methodist by tradition and denomination, and I had learned in my studies about John and Charles Wesley's strong emphasis on the sacraments. John Wesley was willing, even over the objection of his brother and the Anglican Church, to ordain preachers to come to America after the Revolution, primarily so that the American Methodists could have someone to preside over the sacraments. I wondered why something so important to other Christian traditions, to Luther, and to Wesley, seemed so distant and out of mind to the people I worked with, and indeed in my own Christian upbringing and ministry to this point.

I began to do some further reading and talking about the sacraments with other pastors. Eventually, I did a series of classes on the subject with the people in my local church, and we implemented some changes in the way we observed the sacraments in our worship services. No doubt, a lot of the people I was dealing with at the time heard more about the sacraments and learned more about the Lord's Supper than they cared to know. But it was an exciting time of learning and growth for me and for some of the people around me at that time. I look back on that period with fondness, and I recognize the direct impact those days have had on my present ministry and Christian experience.

Out of that has grown this little book. Its purpose is not to present a comprehensive or detailed theological analysis of the sacrament of the Lord's Supper. Volumes could be, and indeed have been, written on each of the topics I discuss here. My basic purpose, instead, is to state concisely those concepts and principles which I have judged through my reading and personal experience to be most basic to an informed understanding and appreciation of the Lord's Supper, particularly from my own tradition as a United Methodist in America. If it will help laypersons and pastors enter into a fuller, more exuberant, more comfortable celebration of the Lord's Supper, then my intentions will have been fulfilled and this small book will have served some worthwhile purpose.

Levon Hucks
Aiken, South Carolina
Lent, 1989

I. Theology

The Lord's Supper as a Meal

Whatever else the Lord's Supper may be, it is, as its name indicates, first and foremost, a meal. As such, it shares with all meals the basic elements of food and drink. Beyond these, it may also share some of the objects of other meals, such as a table and vessels for the food. There are, as well, certain emotions or moods that most meals have in common. They are usually intimate affairs, shared mostly with family and friends. Meals promote fellowship and conversation. These are common, ordinary things that all of us have participated in as we have eaten in our homes, with friends and associates, or with church groups. In these respects, the Lord's Supper is no different from any other meal, and it is from this point of commonality that the Lord's Supper can begin to take on meaning for us. The experiences and objects of other meals, the moods, the emotions—none of these should be left behind when we come to the Lord's Table. Rather, they should inform our experience of it and give us ground, common to every member of the human race, on which to build an understanding of this particular meal.

Perhaps this ordinary, every-day nature of the meal has too often been neglected to our disadvantage. In the early observances of this meal among the followers of Christ, it was the meal itself that was important, not a theological purpose it might serve. The meal came first and then the theologies.

Why should a meal be important to the church? Why has it always been the most characteristic and widely used form of worship among Christians? To answer these questions we need to look at the roots of this meal in the ministry of Jesus and in the Jewish culture in which that ministry took place.

Jewish Meals

For the Jews, every meal was a sacred occasion. It was a time to draw close to God and to one another through the sharing of gifts of food and fellowship around the same table. Meals became meeting places between God and humans as they shared common, ordinary things such as bread, wine, conversation, and stories. Our custom of saying "grace" before the meal comes from the Jewish practice of blessing, or thanking, God for the gifts of food that sustain life.

Meals were also used in the Jewish culture as a sign and seal of covenants. Noah offered food sacrifices to the Lord after his experience on the ark, and God made covenant with Noah never again to destroy the earth and its reproductive ability (Genesis 8:20-22). Similarly, when Moses received the terms of the covenant from God, he went up on a mountain where the covenant was sealed as "they beheld God, and they ate and drank" (Exodus 24:11 NRSV).

As sacred as every meal was to the Jews, the most significant of all meals was the yearly celebration of the Passover meal. Even to this day, at the Passover celebration, the youngest person at the table asks the question, "Why is this night different from all other nights?" The leader responds by telling the story of how God brought the nation of Israel out of slavery in Egypt. He tells the story, not just to remember the past, but to reenact and participate in it at the present moment. The leader says:

> In each generation, every man is duty-bound to envision himself as though he personally took part in the Exodus from Egypt; as we read in the Torah: "You shall tell your son on that day, saying, 'It is because of what the Eternal did for *me* when I came forth from Egypt.' " It was not only our forefathers that the Holy One, blessed be He, redeemed; He redeemed us, the living, together with them. (*From Ashes to Fire*, Abingdon Press, 1979, p. 223)

When we come to the discussion of Jesus' institution of the Lord's Supper, we will see that it works in the same way to make the saving work of Christ a present reality for the church as the Passover meal made the Passover a present reality for the Jews.

Table fellowship was also a sign of hospitality, friendship, and camaraderie to the Jews. They were not only in the presence of God, but also in the presence of one another, and took seriously their commitment to those who sat at their table. In the Near East, more so than in our culture, it is a great act of hostility toward a host to disturb a person seated at his table.

Will Willimon, in his book *Sunday Dinner* (Upper Room, 1981, p. 16), tells the story of a nomad being pursued across the desert by his enemies. The desperate man came upon an encampment where the inhabitants had just begun to eat. He entered the tent where they were seated and stood silent for a moment, until they motioned for him to join them. When his pursuers reached the camp, they entered the same tent ready to seize and kill the man. Finding him seated at the table, they drew back, knowing that in the Near East it is a great act of hostility toward a host and his guest to trouble a person seated at the table. For the time being at least, they had entered into covenant with one another and an insult toward one could bring down the wrath of all the others.

Jesus and Meals

This strong sense of bond between those seated around a common table caused many of the problems Jesus faced with his contemporaries. Jesus welcomed those who were outcast to sit in table-fellowship with him. This was offensive to some of his fellow Jews who accused him of being a glutton and a drunkard, a friend of tax collectors and sinners (Matthew 11:19). He was ridiculed for the type of people he allowed around him and with whom he ate. This table-fellowship with tax collectors and "sinners," in the name of the kingdom of God, could have been so offensive to some of his fellow Jews that it might have led them to hand him over to the Romans to be put to death.

Whether that was the case or not, it is true that the Gospel accounts cast Jesus' ministry in the context of meals and table-fellowship on several occasions (feeding the five thousand and the four thousand, the wedding in Cana, the meal with Zacchaeus, the parables of the prodigal son and the wedding feast, and so forth). One of the most noteworthy, deserving special attention, was that occasion on the night of his passion.

There has been much debate over whether this last meal was a Passover meal (as the Synoptic Gospels would indicate), or whether it took place one night earlier (as John would indicate) and is some other type of meal, possibly a kiddush. My position for this discussion is best expressed in the words of Hans Kung in his book *The Church* (Garden City, N.Y.: Image Books, 1976, p. 279):

Whether it was a Passover meal or not, Jesus' particular words over the bread and wine fitted easily into the ritually ordered course of the Jewish meal: the words over the bread recalling the grace before the main meal, . . . the words over the wine recalling the prayer of thanks. . . . It is probable, therefore, that Jesus took a form which already had religious importance and gave it new content. In this way his words were immediately comprehensible to the disciples.

The Passages of Institution

There are four passages in the New Testament that record what are referred to as the accounts of the institution of the Lord's Supper (Matthew 26:26-29; Mark 14:22-25; Luke 22:15-20, 27-30; and I Corinthians 11:23-26). Three major theological motifs emerge from these four variants of the tradition. First, the Lord's Supper looks back upon an event that has already occurred: the death of Jesus. First Corinthians 11:26 says that when the Lord's Supper is celebrated, it is a present proclamation of a historical event. This acted-out proclamation is not simply a commemorative meal for a dead hero. Jesus' death is proclaimed as having occurred "for" the participants, and its effects are granted to all who celebrate the Supper. The celebrants become participants in his death as they participate in the meal.

The second motif is that of a "present" or "new" proclamation of God's covenant with the church. When the church eats this meal, it is not transported to some faraway time and place by the powers of the mind. Instead, it relives the accomplished saving work of Christ and enters into a present fellowship and covenant with the risen and exalted Lord, and with all the "saints" in all ages and places (communion of the saints). When we eat the bread and drink the cup, we continue a fellowship that began even before Jesus came to Jerusalem to his death, when he ate and drank with his disciples and with tax collectors and "sinners" during his active ministry. It is clear that this meal is intended to do for Christians what the Passover does for Jews as it enables them to relive God's works in history.

The third motif is one of a future anticipation: the messianic banquet that is to occur when the kingdom is fully come. The expectation of a messianic banquet was not a new idea to the Jews. Such a banquet is spoken of in Isaiah 25:6 and 65:13. This banquet is characterized by the joy and jubilation of a feast, not by the sadness of a funeral eulogy. This was certainly the character of the communal meals enjoyed by the New Testament church who "broke bread at home and ate their food with glad and generous hearts, praising God" (Acts 2:46, 47 NRSV).

Post-Resurrection Meals

This so-called Last Supper was not Jesus' last meal, however. He appeared to, and ate with, his disciples on several later occasions (Luke 24:41-43;

John 21:13; Acts 1:4). Most notable was when he appeared to two of his disciples on the road to Emmaus and made himself known to them in the breaking of bread. It is noteworthy that it was not during their discussion, nor during Jesus' teaching, that they recognized him that day. It was, rather, during their table-fellowship that they finally recognized him as he took bread, gave thanks, broke it, and gave it to them—the same basic actions he used at the Last Supper.

Conclusions

When we try to answer why the Lord's Supper has been such an important part of Christian worship over the centuries, we must take all of the aforementioned aspects into account. Though it does have very clear roots in the so-called Last Supper, it also has roots in all the meals Jesus shared with his followers and with tax collectors and "sinners" during his earlier ministry. It has roots in such events as the feeding of the five thousand and the wedding in Cana. It also has strong roots in the post-Resurrection meals Jesus ate with his followers and the promised messianic banquet. All this table-fellowship was characterized by such joy and gladness that it survived the Crucifixion and provided the focal point for the community life and worship of the early church, and for each Christian generation since. There is no reason to believe it should not continue as the focal point of Christian worship until we eat and drink with Christ at his table in his kingdom.

I remember quite vividly a visit I made with an elderly woman in the hospital a few years ago. She was quite ill and had been very disoriented for quite some time. She was conscious and talking, but most of the things she said indicated she had little sense of reality. Her daughter was in the room with her that day, and the daughter and I were talking about her mother's condition when the mother blurted out to her daughter, "Do you know what we did Sunday?" "No, Mama, what did we do Sunday?" she replied. Her mother said, "Those kids went down there on the back of the farm in that nice shady place under the trees and set up a table bigger than this bed. They filled it up with every kind of food you can imagine. Then they came up here and told me they wanted me to come down and eat with them. And I went, knowing I shouldn't. I ate so much I could hardly stand it. We had the best time . . ."

Her daughter and I looked at each other knowingly because we were both aware she had not been out of her hospital room in weeks. But then a description of a scene from Isaiah came to my mind:

Here on Mount Zion the LORD Almighty will prepare a banquet for all the nations of the world—a banquet of the richest food and the finest wine. Here he will sud-

denly remove the cloud of sorrow that has been hang-
ing over all the nations. The Sovereign LORD will
destroy death forever! He will wipe away the tears
from everyone's eyes and take away the disgrace his
people have suffered throughout the world. The LORD
himself has spoken. (Isaiah 25:6-8 TEV)

Maybe she wasn't talking out of her head at all.
Maybe in her own way she did go to a banquet on
Sunday in a cool, shady place on the back of the
farm by a refreshing, running stream. Maybe she
had seen, in images familiar to her, the thing Isaiah
saw on the Mount of the Lord. Perhaps in her delir-
ium she was anticipating that heavenly banquet of
which Isaiah sang.

A few days later, she died.

Just as the Jews recognized both a vertical and a
horizontal relationship in their meals, we also recognize that this continuing fellowship is both with
Christ and also with his people. This fact is clear
from Paul's statement in I Corinthians 10:17:
"Because there is one bread, we who are many are
one body, for we all partake of the one bread"
(NRSV). There is union in the Lord's Supper, union
with Christ and with his people. As we eat this
meal, we fellowship with Christ and with his people, and we proclaim together, until he comes
again, his death on our behalf.

II. HISTORY

Jewish Roots

The history of the Lord's Supper has roots in Jewish worship, especially in synagogue worship, just as the theology of the Lord's Supper has roots in Jewish culture. This connection is to be expected since Jesus and his early followers were Jewish and steeped in Jewish worship practices. It is also true that both Jews and Christians worshiped the same God and that many of the ways Jews worshiped would be acceptable to Christians. All that needed to be done was to "Christianize" these practices.

The focus of the synagogue service was on God, what God had done and what God had promised yet to do. The basic elements were simple: recalling God's acts by reading the history (Scripture) interspersed with psalms (or songs), prayer, and reflection or teaching (sermon). These elements became the first part of the Christian worship service (the "synaxis" or gathering), commonly known as the service of the Word. This service consists of: a greeting in the Lord's name; praise; opening prayers; the reading of the Scriptures interspersed with psalms; teaching and proclamation; affirmations and corporate prayers.

The major Christian addition to the service was the second part known as the service of the Table. Here the focus was upon the sacramental action of the meal. Yet, even though this meal was characteristically Christian, it was also influenced by Jewish practices. We have seen in our discussion of the theology of this meal that the new covenant it proclaims was established in the context of the Passover meal, the climax of the Jewish year. Just as the Passover meal reenacts the deliverance from Egyptian slavery, so also the Lord's Supper reenacts Christ's sacrificial atonement. The thanksgiving prayer of the Lord's Supper is also an adaptation of the prayers of thanksgiving offered in the synagogue for God's saving acts. Thus, we Christians are more Jewish in our worship than is generally realized.

The Early Church

The book of Acts begins with a description of a gathering of the apostles in which Jesus appeared to them after his resurrection and ate with them (1:4). This event forms a link with the stories of post-resurrection meals Jesus ate with his disciples, such as the Emmaus story (Luke 24:13-35). Acts also gives us a brief description of the early communal meals the church shared together.

They devoted themselves to the apostles' teaching and fellowship, to the breaking of bread and the prayers. . . .

Day by day, as they spent much time together in the temple, they broke bread at home and ate their food with glad and generous hearts, praising God and having the goodwill of all the people. (2:42, 46-47a NRSV)

These early observances of the church seem to be full, hunger-satisfying meals characterized by great joy and praise. This joy was not produced primarily by a somber remembrance of the Last Supper, but is probably best explained by their remembrance of their table-fellowship with Jesus both during his active ministry and after his resurrection.

As we saw in our examination of the words of institution at the Last Supper, there is also a future expectation of the messianic banquet when the kingdom is fulfilled. The eucharistic meal, at which Christ is present in the Holy Spirit, is positioned between these past meals and a future banquet. Thus, there is good reason to celebrate.

This is not to say that the Last Supper does not figure into the church's experience of these communal meals from the beginning. In I Corinthians we see a church that seems to have emphasized the celebrative aspect of the communal meal to an extreme, even to the point of drunkenness (11:21). In this case, the church's celebration still appears to be a full meal, and Paul emphasizes that that meal has its origins in the Last Supper. The Last Supper is the source of the meal insofar as it was most likely because of their remembrance of the Last Supper that the disciples gathered to eat after the resurrection

when Christ appeared to them. The disciples probably also remembered in that Last Supper Jesus'
promise of the messianic meal and his promise of
the new covenant established through his death.
When the Corinthian church forgot these things,
Paul felt constrained to emphasize them in his let-
ter to them.

Although it seems clear that the "Lord's supper"
(as Paul calls it in I Corinthians 11:20) was still a full
meal at the time I Corinthians was written, some of
the abuses that may have led to a separation of the
meal and rite are already evident. These abuses at
Corinth arose from pride, selfishness, excesses, and
paganistic influences (10:18-21), which led to fragmentation in the Corinthian church. Paul writes to
them that they are not eating the "Lord's supper"
(κυριακον δειπνον), but their own private supper
(ιδιον δειπνον) to the extent that some eat and drink
to excess while others go hungry. Perhaps they
remembered too well the cultic meals of their pagan
background where the object was to gulp down as
much holy food as possible in order to gain more of
its benefits. Their selfishness, lack of love, and fragmentation are the opposites of the communion
Christ intended for the Lord's Supper to establish.
This church's private, unloving meals are a viola-
tion of "the body of Christ," meaning, in this case,
the church (see I Corinthians 12:12). Paul was led by
such abuses to instruct them to eat at home if they
were hungry before they came together as a church.
Perhaps because of these types of abuses, or the

confusion of the meal with pagan sacred meals (I Corinthians 10:14-22), or the problem of accommodating larger crowds at the meals, the rite was separated from the meal and developed into the ritualized meal as we know it in worship. The full meal (known as the agape) continued as a separate entity. The agape itself was easily abused and fell into disuse. It was revived by some eighteenth-century groups, including Methodists. It also has found some use in ecumenical services in recent years where the Lord's Supper is not feasible. This separation of meal and rite in the Lord's Supper has probably had more impact on the shape of later Christian worship than any other single factor since New Testament times. It seems ironic that we should know so little about exactly when or why it occurred.

When we move beyond this early period in the history of Christian worship and the Lord's Supper, it becomes more complicated. For this discussion, I will group these centuries into the periods of the second and third centuries, the post-Nicene era, the Middle Ages, and post-Reformation. I will emphasize the major changes in the roles of the worship leaders, the people, and the meal itself.

Second and Third Centuries

In the second and third centuries, the worship of the church became more structured and defined.

Justin's *Apologia* (A.D. 150) describes the worship of this period as taking place on the Lord's Day (Sunday) and as being led by worship leaders called "presidents." There appears to have been no distinction in the status of clergy and laity at this point. The president delivered the sermon after the readings from Scripture and presided at the Lord's Supper, generally called the "Eucharist" (Thanksgiving) during this period. One of the president's most important functions was his ability to lead the congregation in this eucharistic prayer. The themes of the prayer were fixed, but the actual wording was left to the one who prayed. This prayer was the most common theological statement of the Christian faith. Having been set in charge of leading this prayer, the president was made the resident theologian for the congregation.

The emphasis upon the congregation was that of participation. Though they did not pray as the president led, they responded to the prayer and showed their assent with the "Amen." There was no distinction in status between the worship leaders and the congregation at this point. They were a community, but they were a defined community. Only the baptized and instructed believers were allowed to participate in the Eucharist. There was no open communion in this period.

The meal itself, as characterized by the eucharistic prayers written by Hippolytus (a second-century bishop), was one of joyful triumph at the victory of Christ. There was little emphasis on the Passion and suffering of Jesus. This meal was not a funeral meal for a departed hero, but the resurrection meal of an exalted Lord. It was joyful and future-oriented, looking forward to a new day of redemption of all creation. This future hope was a present reality rightfully appropriated by all who partook of this joyful meal.

The elements used at the meal were gifts brought by members of the congregation. They were ordinary leavened table bread and wine. It was much later that unleavened bread was used, and later still that unfermented grape juice became popular.

Post-Nicene Era

During the post-Nicene era, several liturgical families or styles developed, centered in different geographical areas. In the West there were two main families, the Gallic and the Roman. The Gallic rites were characterized by a high degree of congregational participation, ceremonies rich in symbolism and drama, and prayer that was poetic and flowing. The Roman rites were more simple, formal, and restrained. There was little congregational involvement. Eventually the Roman rite took precedent over all others in the West.

In the Roman rites of this period, the clergy took on a new prominence. Distinctions were made between clergy and laity, and the clergy were in

charge of the liturgy. As the clergy gained prominence, the laity became less involved in the service
and became spectators instead of participants. The
service itself became more cluttered with peripher-
al concerns so that the eucharistic prayer was more
complex and less unified. The Eucharist and the
Liturgy of the Word became known as the "Mass,"
a term that comes from the dismissal at the end of
the service (*Ite missa est*—"you are dismissed"). It
emphasizes the idea of sacrifice, focusing on the
words of institution. This sacrificial tone, coupled
with the prominence of the clergy, resulted in the
Mass becoming a priestly sacrifice that had lost
much of its sense of joyful thanksgiving.

The Middle Ages

During the Middle Ages these trends were
extended. There was a total separation between
clergy and people. The liturgy was conducted in
Latin, a language understood only by the priest,
and so the laity were almost totally deprived of
participation. They only saw the liturgy performed
as they went about their private and subjective
devotions. The tone of the liturgy was increasingly
penitential and introspective, with more emphasis
upon each celebration as a separate sacrificial offering, related to Calvary, but having a value entirely
on its own. It was during this period that the doc-

trine of transubstantiation developed, which states that the elements become the actual body and blood of Christ at the reciting of the words of institution. This doctrine made the service even more awesome and led to the use of pure white wafers and the taking of the cup from the laity.

Reformation and Post-Reformation

During the Reformation and following, some attempts were made to reform some of the abuses of previous centuries. There was still a high degree of emphasis on subjective, penitential devotions and on the sacrificial nature of the Lord's Supper. The clergy took a lesser role, and there were attempts at restoring congregational participation. Martin Luther's major contribution was the addition of vernacular hymnody and liturgy. He attempted to restore weekly communion but, for a people used to annual celebrations, this was too much. The sermon, instead, gained prominence and became the focus of weekly worship. Zwingli took a more radical view than did Luther. He gave the Scriptures supreme and sole authority and had little use for the sacramental aspects of worship. He rejected the Lord's Supper as the normal focus of weekly worship and instituted quarterly celebrations. Calvin, on the other hand, had a high doctrine of the sacraments and advocated the Lord's

Supper as the weekly focus of worship. He, like Luther, was unsuccessful.

John Wesley's Contributions

John Wesley came on the scene a couple of centuries later in England. Though he brought no new theological statement on the sacraments, he did make three significant contributions: a revival of weekly celebrations and a renewal of participation; the drawing together of sacrament and evangelism; and (along with his brother Charles) the creation of a rich collection of 166 eucharistic hymns. Wesley drew attention to the Lord's Supper as a means of evangelism, a "converting ordinance" as he called it. He stressed that, as a means of grace and as a command of Christ, the Lord's Supper should be celebrated at every opportunity when the worshiping community came together. He and Charles made the joyful celebration of it possible and furthered the laity's theological understanding of the Eucharist with their rich collection of hymns.

American Methodism

Wesley's eucharistic disciplines and eucharistic hymns were not greatly appreciated by his followers, especially in America, where the dominant emphasis was "revivalistic." The perceived need on the frontier was for evangelism. In the revivals of the Great Awakening of the eighteenth century, the emphasis was on preaching and singing. The focus was on entry into faith, with little emphasis on the long-term nurture of the faith or on the sacraments. The sermon was the focus, not just of the revivals, but also of weekly worship; and not just in Methodism, but in most Protestant worship in America.

There was a further problem that led to the neglect of the sacraments in American Methodism—the lack of ordained clergy to administer the sacraments. Wesley was an ordained Anglican priest and remained Anglican for life. He was strongly opposed to separating his Methodist classes from the Anglican Church into their own denomination. It was inevitable, however, that this should happen, especially in America, if not before his death, then after. But Wesley had no authority to ordain clergy, and he refused to allow unordained persons to preside at the sacraments. This was no real problem in England, where Anglican churches and ministers were abundant, but it was on the American frontier, where the preachers (ordained or not) were few and scattered. The Methodist Church in America, therefore, grew up without much exposure to the Lord's Supper or to Wesley's emphasis on weekly communion. The Methodist bodies in America have never gotten over this early unfamiliarity with the Lord's Supper.

American Protestantism

There are other developments that have had a profound influence on the Lord's Supper in most of American Protestantism: the use of individual wafers and glasses, and the use of unfermented grape juice instead of wine. The custom of using individual pressed wafers is an extension of medieval practices brought on by a preoccupation with the bread as the actual body of Christ. There was a fear of desecrating it by dropping crumbs on the floor or chewing the body of Christ. The custom of using individual glasses appears to have grown out of the Scottish Presbyterian desire to recover the meal of the Last Supper by giving the participants individual cups and small buns and seating them around the table. The glasses and wafers got smaller while the modern preoccupation with germs and hygiene grew larger. In recent years, the fear and paranoia generated by the rise of the AIDS virus has magnified this preoccupation.

We have also seen (within the past hundred years) a switch in about three quarters of the Protestant churches from wine to grape juice. This shift is presumably related to the high concern expressed in this country for total abstinence from alcoholic beverages (a concern that led to the Volstead Act, establishing prohibition). Another factor is the concern about tempting reformed alcoholics. Thus, the celebration of the Lord's Supper in American Protestant churches for at least the last hundred years has been characterized by the use of pressed wafers or small pieces of bread, individual cups, and grape juice. These customs have been affected, however, by recent tendencies in American Protestantism toward liturgical renewal. This renewal is spawned largely by increased information and study of early worship practices, and the impetus for liturgical reform generated by Vatican II in the Roman Catholic Church.

III. Symbol

Introduction

Any research into the symbolic nature of the Lord's Supper will include an examination of more than the symbolic elements of bread and wine. It will also have to include a consideration of the nature of symbols and sacraments, the sign-acts associated with the sacrament, the setting for the sacrament, and even the names that are used to refer to the sacrament.

Signs

Paul Tillich, in his book *Dynamics of Faith* (Harper, 1957, pp. 41-43), makes a distinction between symbols and signs that is helpful at this point for the sake of clarity. A sign is a pointer that is arbitrary and always represents a thing signified. This would be the case with the scientific designation for water, H_2O. H_2O signifies nothing else but water and will always point beyond itself to this reality, yet it has nothing to do with the reality of water itself. A symbol is different in that it participates in the reality of that to which it points. It is not the equivalent of what it represents, but it does somehow participate in the quality and character of the thing symbolized. The symbol evokes a level of reality and perception that cannot adequately or fully be expressed by any other means. With symbols we may see levels of reality we could not, or did not, see before. Bread and wine are not the same as body and blood, but as symbols used in the Lord's Supper they can represent and involve one in the reality of Christ's broken body and shed blood in a way that would be impossible without symbols.

The church has a vast array of symbols: the cross, the dove, the fish, tongues of fire, waters of baptism, and the bread and wine of communion. The supreme symbol for the church, however, is Jesus. He is the reality of God in visible, tangible form. Yet he is not visible to the church today. Therefore who and what he was is passed on to the modern church in other symbols, which convey the reality of God in Christ, living among humanity. These symbols are the words, acts, and objects that make up what we call sacraments.

Sacraments

The sacraments are God's way of showing forth his love to humanity in visible and tangible forms. The reality behind the words, actions, and objects of the Christian sacraments is God's love for humanity. Sacraments attempt to make that love visible and tangible to modern humanity as Christ made God's love visible and tangible to first-century humanity. The sacraments can be viewed as extensions of the incarnation. All the reality of God's self-giving love, of Christ's living and dying, his resurrection and ascension, his present reality, and the hope of his coming again is made visible and available to modern humanity in the sacraments. It is here, in the waters of baptism, and (for this study particularly) in the bread and wine of the Lord's Supper, that God meets humanity. The sacraments invite us to taste, see, hear, smell, touch, and feel that the Lord is good (Psalm 34:8).

The reality involved in the sacraments is not only vertical (God-to-humanity), but also horizontal (person-to-person). The sacraments have no meaning or function outside of the community of people who interact with them. The sacraments not only allow God to relate to the community, but they allow the community to relate to one another and to build one another up in love, faith, and hope. The sacraments do this by both enabling the community to establish new relationships of love, and by maintaining and nourishing existing relationships. The sacraments invite people to interact with God and one another, and by so doing, to experience God's love and share it among themselves.

The word sacrament deserves some explanation. The Greek word is μυστηριον, meaning "secret" or "mystery" (in the sense of something formerly unknown but now revealed). It is used to refer to the secret (or mysterious) thoughts (or nature) of God which transcend human reason and comprehension and which must therefore be revealed by God. When applied to those rites which we know as the sacraments, the term refers to God's revelation of God's self and God's love to the church.

Our English word *sacrament* is derived from the Latin word *sacramentum*, used to translate the Greek μυστηριον. The word had two common meanings: (1) a pledge deposited in public keeping by the parties in a lawsuit and forfeited to a sacred purpose; and (2) an oath of allegiance taken by a soldier. These two ideas later combined to create the concept of a sacred rite that was a solemn pledge. It is a more legalistic term than μυστηριον and more limited in terms of conveying the vastness of God's self-giving. An exact definition of a sacrament is not essential, however. This need for exactness and specificity is a modern phenomenon. In the early church the sacraments were more experienced than debated. The need for experience of these mysteries is still more important than complete understanding. There is no higher level of expression for the mystery of a sacrament than what we experience in the sacrament itself.

The Lord's Supper

There has never been any question that the Lord's Supper is a sacrament, though there has never been complete agreement as to what constitutes a sacrament or how many sacraments there are. The Lord's Supper is the most widely experienced mystery of God's self-revelation to humanity. Indeed, it has been the characteristic form that most Christian worship has taken through the centuries. Yet its mystery goes far beyond human abilities of comprehension. Its many facets are reflected in the many titles used to refer to this sacrament: Eucharist, Lord's Supper, Holy Communion, Mass, Service of the Table, and others. Each one of these titles emphasizes a slightly different aspect (for example, Eucharist—thanksgiving; Lord's Supper—meal or the Lord's meal; Communion—fellowship and unity); yet none conveys the fullness of its meaning by itself.

Pastoral concerns compel those charged with the administering of this sacrament to God's people to allow it to speak in its fullness as far as possible. We can examine the possibilities for a full celebration of the Lord's Supper by looking into two areas: the setting and the actions.

The Setting

Basic to the Lord's Supper is the meal. Most meals have a domestic intimacy, yet many of our architectural settings make the expression of this intimacy difficult. Many of our churches are too large or are built according to medieval or secular standards and limit our possibilities. Nevertheless, in preparing a meal or banquet for God's people, certain elements are necessary.

Every meal calls for a table. The design of this table and its setting can say much about the nature of our meal. Many altar-tables are placed far away from the congregation, in a chancel, many of these up against, or built into, the wall. Such a setting dictates that the leader stand far from the people and turn his back to them at significant times during the meal. It seems best that the table be free-standing so that the minister can face the people, the guests of the meal. It also should be close enough to the people so that the minister can be seen and heard easily.

The form of the table can vary. It would seem logical that its size fit its use among the people, and not be scaled to the size of the building. Its form should also suggest its use both as a place where a meal is served and as a place where praise, prayer, and thanksgiving are offered. The sacrificial nature of Christ's offering in union with these offerings of the church may best be conveyed by a table that suggests that it is also an altar.

We must also keep the people in mind when planning our meal. They should be treated as participants and not only be faced by the leader, but should also find it easy to gather at the table. This could best be done if the people could sit around the table, but this is too limiting for the other functions of the church. Therefore, a compromise is often made and the people are brought up to the table, either to stand, kneel, or sit, depending on the nature of the occasion and the size of the group. Being able to gather at the table supports the sense of fellowship and unity among the body.

The Action

The Lord's Supper involves four basic actions. These are the same as those Jesus used in the Emmaus story: "When he was at table with them, he took bread, blessed and broke it, and gave it to them" (Luke 24:30 NRSV). The first action is Jesus' *taking bread.* This is the action of preparation for the meal. In the early worship of the church, particularly when the Lord's Supper was a full meal, the entire congregation contributed bread and wine, which was collected and used for the sacrament. Along with these food items, collections of money were received for the relief of the poor. There is no reason why the church could not continue this practice, contributing not only gifts of money, but also gifts of real bread and wine to be used in the sacrament.

Next, Jesus *blessed* the bread. In a domestic meal, we would call this "saying grace" or "asking the blessing." This is the only part of the sacrament that is mostly verbal, but the words can also be accompanied by sign-acts, especially during the recitation of the words of institution. The purpose of this portion of the meal is simply to thank God for his many works and gifts. It is the prayer of the people, led by the minister, which the people should take part in, at least by the "Amen" of agreement at the end.

The *breaking* of the bread is actually a utilitarian act that also has significant sign value, especially when accompanied by the words of Paul comparing the unity of the loaf with the unity of the body, and the partaking of that broken loaf with a participation in the atoning effects of Christ's death (I Corinthians 10:16, 17). In this action it becomes clear that the elements of bread and wine, and the form in which they are present, are an important part of the action. Continuity with the biblical tradition, the early church, and subsequent Christian tradition would call for the use of bread and wine alone as the proper elements of this meal, instead of remythologizing the Supper so that any ordinary food would do (such as soft drinks and potato chips). If the Lord's Supper is celebrated in connection with the agape meal, however, this would provide an opportunity for using many other kinds of food along with the bread and wine. Considering these two elements, the bread cannot be broken with full sign value unless it is a loaf of whole bread, large enough to be held and broken in the view of the people. The cup also cannot have its full sign value unless it looks like a drinking cup and contains real wine. Nothing is more indicative of disunity and fragmentation in the church than the modern custom of using individual cubes of bread or wafers, and small individual cups of watered-down grape juice. On the other hand, the symbols of one loaf, which we all eat, and one cup, from which we all drink, are the most powerful symbols of the unity of the body that the church possesses.

The *giving* of the bread and wine are the final sign-acts of the sacrament. The climax of the service (as in any meal) comes when it is time to eat and drink. It is the time for action. It will probably call for the people to get up and come to the table. This in itself can be an act of dedication and commitment, and unity as well, as the people come together to the same table to eat of the same loaf and drink of the same cup. The act of giving, as opposed to "taking," has sign value. The people of God do not take the gifts of God. The gifts are given by God (the minister acting as God's representative), and the people receive them. The giving of the cup poses particular problems in our germ-conscious modern culture. The use of a common cup has a greater sign value of unity and carries little danger of contamination when wiped and turned after each communicant. However, considering the present mind-set of most Americans, it may be best to provide an alternative to drinking from the same cup. Some may be willing to dip their bread into the cup (intinction) to preserve the sign value. The method with the least sign value (except perhaps negative sign value) is the use of individual cups, unless perhaps the wine is poured from a common pitcher into each individual's cup, but this is possible only in small settings.

Conclusions

These are the basic elements of the sacrament of the Lord's Supper. Since symbols, actions, and words are basic to the nature of a sacrament, it is very important that these elements be expressed so that the sacrament may best show forth the mystery of God's self-giving love. The Sacrament must be allowed its full expression so that it conveys to us the message God would have us perceive.

POSTSCRIPT

There are certain convictions that I have formulated in the course of my dealing with this subject that need some comment.

First, the Lord's Supper is the normative pattern of Christian worship. It is the uniquely Christian pattern and ought to be celebrated each Lord's Day. The full service of Word and Table has been the chief form of worship for the vast majority of Christianity since the earliest days of the church. This is still true today, from the Eastern Orthodox Church to the Churches of Christ. It was intended by John Wesley to be true of Methodism, but that has not been the case. It is imperative for the worship life of The United Methodist Church (and others like us in this respect) to restore at least weekly celebrations of the Eucharist. It may be possible to do this by alternating between morning or evening services, between Sunday and mid-week services, or (in larger churches) between an early morning and later morning service.

Second, the Lord's Supper proclaims the entire span of the gospel and the saving work of Christ. This includes not only his death, but also his life and ministry, his passion, his resurrection, his post-resurrection appearances, his present covenant with us, and the expectation of the eschatological messianic banquet. Too much emphasis has been placed on the somber passion and death of Christ and a penitential mood of "celebration." The Eucharist should be a thankful celebration of all the saving work of Christ in all places and all ages.

Third, the Lord's Supper is basically action and symbol, not words. These symbols and actions witness to the unity of the body as the people of the church gather around the table of their common Lord. All the actions and symbols of the Eucharist should give witness to the corporate nature of this sacrament. Nothing works contrary to this unity more than our use of fragmented symbols like individual cups and wafers or cubes of bread. These symbols should be restored to the common cup from which we all can drink and the common loaf from which we all can eat.

Fourth, basic to the Lord's Supper is the meal. Whenever possible, churches should restore the full service of Word, Meal, and Rite. At the very least, real bread and real wine should be used at every celebration of the Lord's Supper and these should be given in sufficient quantities for the celebrants to know they have had real food and real drink as they would at any meal. Reclaiming this rich symbolism should go a long way toward a recovery of the joyful fellowship of the eucharistic feast.

Last, the Lord's Supper belongs to the worshiping community and not to the clergy. At every opportunity the congregation should be invited to participate: in the offering of gifts (especially the bread and wine), in the prayer of thanksgiving, in the gathering around the table to receive the gifts of God, in the actual administration of the gifts, and so on. Perhaps it is best for the prayer of thanksgiving to be prayed by a clergyperson as the leader of the congregation charged with the expression of the church's faith. But the celebrants should be invited to join in by the use of printed or memorized responses and to indicate their consent with the "Amen." Laypersons should also be allowed to assist in the administration of the elements to the rest of the congregation. The lay leader would seem an obvious choice among United Methodists, but not exclusively so.

These five themes appear to me to be central to the Lord's Supper and necessary for the Eucharist to make its full impact upon the worshiping community. The purpose of this book has been to state why I believe this to be so and to encourage pastors and congregations to make these ideals realities. There has been much renewal in the area of worship and sacraments in recent years, much of it misunderstood by clergy and by people in the pews. I hope this book is small enough not to intimidate anyone, so that people will read it, yet sound enough in its theology, conclusions, and application that it will assist in an honest and welcomed revival of the Lord's Supper among our congregations. I am convinced such a revival is very much needed, and that if it could be accomplished, it could help to raise up a more mature, "worshipful" generation of believers.

A Case Study

I met Candy when she was one of the adult counselors with the youth program at my first pastorate. She had become involved with the church through her husband, who grew up in that church. Ironically, he no longer attended, but they had a teenage son and daughter whom Candy was anxious to have involved in the church, so she brought them to Sunday school and worship, and became one of the counselors to the youth program. It was a small group of youth, but she and the other counselors worked hard to do the best they could for and with the youth.

About two years after I got to know Candy, her husband died suddenly at a young age. I worked with her and her two children on the funeral services and tried to help them deal with their grief as best I could. During this time I met Candy's brother and mother, and I continued to develop a closeness to, and appreciation for, the entire family.

About a year later Candy met Joe at work. Joe's wife had died recently as well. Joe was a committed Christian who came to worship with Candy regularly. It was obvious they cared for each other very much, so I was not surprised when they came to see me and asked me to help them plan and conduct their wedding.

In subsequent consultations with Joe and Candy, I talked with them about the form of the wedding ceremony itself. We discussed the traditional ceremony, but we also looked at the Service of Christian Marriage in what was then called the "Supplemental Worship Resources" of The United Methodist Church. We talked about Christian marriage as worship and the appropriateness of celebrating the Lord's Supper in the marriage ceremony. Candy and Joe seemed interested in these ideas, and over the next few weeks we decided together to base the wedding ceremony on the Word and Table pattern used in the Supplemental Resources. I put together an order of worship and, with some adjustments at Candy and Joe's suggestion, we settled on the ritual for the ceremony.

We intended that the wedding would be brief, but that it would be a full service of worship with hymns, prayers, Scripture, and sacrament. Candy and Joe provided the wine and bread. The bread was homemade. The wine was a good quality red port purchased locally.

On the day of the wedding, I came out a few minutes before the service and spoke to the congregation about the nature of the service, since it might be unfamiliar to many of them. I especially emphasized their participation in the service and the role each one of them played. Then we briefly "walked through" the service as it was printed in the bulletin each had been given.

During the service I read the story of creation of man and woman from Genesis 2:18-25, and the story of Jesus' visit to the wedding feast in Cana of Galilee in John 2:1-11. I then charged Candy and Joe, and the congregation, before God based on these texts. And then the vows were exchanged.

For the Communion, I served Candy and Joe first. Then Joe assisted me in distributing the elements to the rest of the wedding party and, after that, to the congregation. We invited people to make their way to the Communion rail at their own pace, and to stand to be served as a sign of joy and thanksgiving for the marriage of Joe and Candy.

When everyone had been served, the husband and wife embraced each other, and the "Peace" was passed among the people of the congregation. Joe and Candy then remained in the sanctuary while family and friends greeted them and gave them their blessing. Later, all who wished to stay gathered downstairs in the Fellowship Hall where we laughed, talked, and ate until everyone was satisfied and the time came for Joe and Candy to leave.

I had done many weddings before and have done many since, and all of them have had their special qualities. But none has impressed me with quite the same spiritual satisfaction and joy as the wedding of Joe and Candy. It was partly because of the friendship we shared. But it was largely, I am convinced, because of the unreserved way in which Candy and Joe celebrated their marriage as an act of worship in the full context of Word and Table. I am glad for whatever service I might have been able to render to Joe and Candy. But I don't think they yet fully realize the gift which they gave to me and to that congregation in their wedding. It was truly an act of worship.

Letter from John Wesley

To Dr. COKE, Mr. ASBURY, and our Brethren in NORTH-AMERICA.

1. By a very uncommon train of providences, many of the provinces of *North-America* are totally disjoined from their mother-country, and erected into Independent States. The English government has no authority over them either civil or ecclesiastical, any more than over the States of *Holland.* A civil authority is exercised over them, partly by the Congress, partly by the provincial Assemblies. But no one either exercises or claims any ecclesiastical authority at all. In this peculiar situation some thousands of the inhabitants of these States desire my advice; and in compliance with their desire, I have drawn up a little sketch.

2. Lord KING'S account of the primitive church convinced me many years ago, that Bishops and Presbyters are the same order, and consequently have the same right to ordain. For many years I have been importuned from time to time, to exer-

cise this right, by ordaining part of our travelling preachers. But I have still refused, not only for peace' sake: but because I was determined, as little as possible to violate the established order of the national church to which I belonged.

3. But the case is widely different between England and North-America. Here there are Bishops who have a legal jurisdiction. In America there are none, neither any parish ministers. So that for some hundred miles together there is none either to baptize or to administer the Lord's Supper. Here therefore my scruples are at an end: and I conceive myself at full liberty, as I violate no order and invade no man's right, by appointing and sending labourers into the harvest.

4. I have accordingly appointed Dr. COKE and Mr. FRANCIS ASBURY, to be joint *Superintendents* over our brethren in North-America: As also RICHARD WHATCOAT and THOMAS VASEY, to act as *Elders* among them, by baptizing and administering the Lord's Supper. And I have prepared a liturgy little differing from that of the church of England (I think, the best constituted national church in the world) which I advise all the travelling-preachers to use, on the Lord's day, in all their congregations, reading the litany only on Wednesdays and Fridays, and praying extempore on all other days. I also advise the elders to administer the supper of the Lord on every Lord's day.

5. If any one will point out a more rational and scriptural way, of feeding and guiding those poor

sheep in the wilderness, I will gladly embrace it. At present I cannot see any better method than I have taken.

6. It has indeed been proposed, to desire the English Bishops, to ordain part of our preachers for *America*. But to this I object, 1. I desired the Bishop of *London,* to ordain only one; but could not prevail: 2. If they consented, we know the slowness of their proceedings; but the matter admits of no delay. 3. If they would ordain them *now,* they would likewise expect to govern them. And how grievously would this intangle us? 4. As our *American* brethren are now totally disentangled both from the State, and from the English Hierarchy, we dare not intangle them again, either with the one or the other. They are now at full liberty, simply to follow the scriptures and the primitive church. And we judge it best that they should stand fast in that liberty, wherewith GOD has so strangely made them free. JOHN WESLEY.

A Suggested
Study Guide

In preparation, write a paragraph describing what the Lord's Supper means to you. Put it aside or in an envelope and seal it. Also, get a copy or copies of your church's bulletin or order of worship.

I. Theology.

1. Think about meals you have eaten—with family, in social settings, in religious settings. What is common to each of these? What is different?

2. Recall, as close to chronological order as possible, the role of food and meals in the events of the Old Testament. What patterns or themes do you notice?

3. Recall instances in Jesus' ministry that included food or meals. What patterns or themes emerge?

4. Look at the passages of institution in the Gospels and I Corinthians as given in the text (p. 18). What are the past, present, and future dimensions of these texts and this event?

5. Read Luke 24:13-35. What is the climax of this passage, and how do the events build up to it? When did the disciples recognize who this stranger was? Why? What order of worship

might you put together based on the pattern of events in this passage? Compare to the order of worship used in your church. Compare to that found in the new *United Methodist Hymnal* (1989).

In preparation for section II, read John Wesley's sermon "The Duty of Constant Communion," found in collections of his sermons. See Sources and Suggestions for Further Reading at the back of this book for bibliographic information.

II. History

1. Read I Corinthians 11:17-34. What does Paul say that suggests he is talking about a full meal? What was going on at these meals that displeased Paul? What does Paul mean by "the body" of Christ (v. 29)? What, then, was their sin? How might this sin have contributed to the separation of meal and rite?

2. Consider the historical periods traced in the text. How do each of the following change and develop during these periods: the leader's role, the bread and wine, the congregation's role?

3. What were the contributions and emphases of John Wesley with regard to the Lord's Supper? How are these evident or not evident in modern United Methodism? In your church?

4. In which historical period would you most have liked to worship, and why?

III. Symbol

1. What are the similarities and differences between signs and symbols?
2. What is a sacrament?
3. What are the symbols and symbolic actions of the sacrament of the Lord's Supper as you have experienced it?
4. Recall the various names given to the Lord's Supper. What are the one or two main characteristics conveyed by each name?
5. How does the message communicated vary if the sanctuary is pulpit-centered or altar-centered? If the Lord's Supper is served around the table or in the pews? If the Lord's Supper is served from a common cup or individual cups? If the elements are wine and home-made bread or grape juice and processed wafers?
6. What changes would you make in the way the Lord's Supper is celebrated in your church if you could?

Write a paragraph describing what the Lord's Supper means to you. Compare with the paragraph you wrote and put away before reading and discussing this material.

Sources and Suggestions for Further Reading

The Apostolic Tradition of Hippolytus. Trans. Burron Scott Eston. Hamden, Connecticut: Archon Books, 1962.

Bowmer, John C. *The Lord's Supper in Methodism: 1791–1960*. London: Epworth Press, 1961.

Cullman, Oscar. *Early Christian Worship*. Trans. A. Stewart Todd and James B. Torrance. London: SCM Press, 1953.

Dix, Dom Gregory. *The Shape of the Liturgy*. Westminster: Dacre Press, 1945.

Garrett, I. S. *Christian Worship*. 2nd ed. London: Oxford University Press, 1963.

Hatchett, Marion J. *Sanctifying Life, Time and Space: An Introduction to Liturgical Study*. New York: Seabury Press, 1976.

Hickman, Hoyt; Saliers, D. F.; Stookey, L. H.; and White, J. F. *Handbook of the Christian Year*. Nashville: Abingdon Press, 1986.

Hickman, Hoyt. *A Primer for Church Worship*. Nashville: Abingdon Press, 1984.

Jeremias, Joachim. *The Eucharistic Words of Jesus*. New York: Charles Scribner's Sons, 1966.

John Wesley's Sunday Service of the Methodists in North America. Introduction by James F. White. Nashville: The United Methodist Publishing House and the United Methodist Board of Higher Education, 1984.

Luther, Martin. *Martin Luther: Selections from His Writings*. Ed. John Dillenberger. Garden City, N.Y.: Doubleday, 1961.

MacDonald, Alexander B. *Christian Worship in the Primitive Church*. Edinburgh: T & T Clark, 1935.

Martin, Ralph P. *Worship in the Early Church*. Grand Rapids: William B. Eerdmans, 1964.

Perrin, Norman. *Rediscovering the Teaching of Jesus*. New York: Harper & Row, 1976.

Rattenburg, J. Ernest. *The Eucharistic Hymns of John and Charles Wesley*. London: Epworth Press, 1948.

Schweizer, Eduard. *The Lord's Supper According to the New Testament*. Trans. James M. Davis. Facet Books Biblical Series, No. 18. Philadelphia: Fortress Press, 1967.

Sovik, E. A. *Architecture for Worship*. Minneapolis: Augsburg, 1973.

Wesley, John. "The Duty of Constant Communion." *The Works of John Wesley*. vol. VII, pp. 147-57. London: Wesleyan Methodist Book Room, 1872; reprint ed., Grand Rapids: Baker Book House, 1978.

White, James F. *Christian Worship in Transition*. Nashville: Abingdon Press, 1976.

_____. *Introduction to Christian Worship*. Nashville: Abingdon Press, 1980.

_____. *New Forms of Worship*. Nashville: Abingdon Press, 1971.

Willimon, William H. *Sunday Dinner: The Lord's Supper and the Christian Life*. Educational Introduction by John Westerhoff III. Nashville: The Upper Room, 1981.

_____. *Word, Water, Wine and Bread: How Worship Has Changed Over the Years*. Valley Forge: Judson Press, 1980.

_____. *Worship as Pastoral Care*. Nashville: Abingdon Press, 1979.